# The Ultimate Keto Desserts Cookbook

50 Keto Desserts Recipes to Make at Home

# Table of Contents

INTRODUCTION ........................................................................................................................... 4
CREAM CHEESE KETO POUND CAKE ..................................................................................... 6
KETO MINT BROWNIES ............................................................................................................. 8
KETO PATRIOTIC DESSERT - CHEESECAKE MOUSSE ....................................................... 10
KETO BIG MAC SAUCE ............................................................................................................ 12
DELICIOUS LOW CARB SCUFFINS - CARBQUIK ................................................................ 14
SPICY MAYO - KOREAN MAYONNAISE ............................................................................... 16
KETO BLACKBERRY COCONUT BAKE ................................................................................. 18
PUMPKIN CHEESECAKE MOUSSE ......................................................................................... 20
HIGH PROTEIN JELLO MOUSSE ............................................................................................. 22
KETO CHOCOLATE CHAFFLES .............................................................................................. 24
RASPBERRY CREAM BOMBS .................................................................................................. 26
KETO MILKY CHOCOLATE TRUFFLES ................................................................................. 28
INSTANT POT THAI COCONUT PANDAN CUSTARD .......................................................... 30
MEXICAN HOT CHOCOLATE MIX ......................................................................................... 32
STEVIA SWEETENED BLUEBERRY FRUIT LEATHER ........................................................ 34
LOW CARB KETO STRAWBERRY SHORTCAKE ................................................................. 36
MATCHA GREEN TEA CHIA PUDDING ................................................................................. 38
HOMEMADE BUTTERSCOTCH PUDDING ............................................................................ 40
GLUTEN-FREE TIRAMISU WHOOPIE PIES – LOW CARB .................................................. 42
EASY DOUBLE CHOCOLATE CHAFFLES ............................................................................. 45
KETO CHAFFLE GARLIC CHEESY BREAD STICKS ............................................................ 47
LOW-CARB DARK CHERRY CRUNCH PIE ........................................................................... 49
KETO GOLDEN MILK ICE CREAM ......................................................................................... 51
KETO MIXED BERRY CRUMBLE ........................................................................................... 53
KETO MINI PECAN PIES ........................................................................................................... 55
WORLD'S GREATEST LOW CARB KETO WAFFLES ........................................................... 57
LOW CARB SEMIFREDDO ....................................................................................................... 59
KETO CANNOLI CHEESECAKE .............................................................................................. 61
KETO DALGONA COFFEE – WHIPPED COFFEE .................................................................. 63
LOW CARB ITALIAN CREAM CAKE ..................................................................................... 65

- KETO BROWNIE MUFFINS ............................................................................................... 68
- KETO GRAHAM CRACKERS .............................................................................................. 70
- KETO CHOCOLATE DIPPED STRAWBERRIES ..................................................................... 72
- NO-BAKE KETO PEANUT BUTTER CHOCOLATE BARS ...................................................... 74
- KETO BAGEL FAT BOMBS ................................................................................................. 76
- BLACKBERRY COCONUT FAT BOMBS ............................................................................... 78
- KETO PINA COLADA FAT BOMBS ..................................................................................... 80
- LOW-CARB CHOCOLATE MESS WITH BERRIES AND CREAM ........................................... 82
- KETO BAKED GOAT CHEESE WITH BLACKBERRIES AND ROASTED PISTACHIOS ............. 85
- KETO FRENCH PANCAKES ................................................................................................. 87
- LOW-CARB BAKED APPLES ............................................................................................... 89
- OLD-FASHIONED KETO CAKE DONUTS ............................................................................ 91
- SUGAR-FREE RASPBERRY CHOCOLATE SOUFFLÉ ............................................................. 93
- LOW-CARB STRAWBERRY CREAM GUMMIES .................................................................. 95
- LOW-CARB GRANOLA BARS ............................................................................................. 97
- SALTY CHOCOLATE TREAT ................................................................................................ 99
- KETO BUÑUELOS ............................................................................................................. 101
- LOW-CARB FROZEN YOGURT POPSICLES ....................................................................... 103
- LOW-CARB CRANBERRY CREAM WITH PECANS ............................................................ 105
- LOW-CARB CHEESE PLATTER ......................................................................................... 107

# INTRODUCTION

*All of the tastiest ketos treat in one spot! From fudgy keto brownies to luscious sugar-free ice cream to special occasion layer cakes, there's something for everyone. Do you have a need for keto cookies that taste just like genuine? Yes, we have those as well. It's not for nothing that I'm known as the "Keto Dessert Queen."*

*Let's face it: not every keto dessert dish is created equal. You don't want to waste your time or money on desserts and snacks that don't measure up to their expectations. You're looking for tried-and-true recipes that don't taste like they're low-carb.*

*You want sweets that will wow even the most avowed carbohydrate aficionado. You're looking for keto sweets that no one will notice are healthy. You don't have to tell them unless* you want to. That is all up to you, my friend. It's possible that it'll be our little secret.

We've made it our aim in life to develop low-carb sweets that taste just as wonderful, if not better, than the genuine thing, as a dedicated baker who has lived with diabetes for the past eight years. However, over the last few years, we've gradually reduced my carb intake and totally embraced the ketogenic lifestyle. This blog's content isn't entirely keto-friendly.

So, we went through all of my dozens of recipes in search of desserts that fit the keto diet the best.

All of my best dessert recipes with less than 10g total carbs may be found here. These keto dessert recipes are designed to fit in well with your macros.

# CREAM CHEESE KETO POUND CAKE

*Prep Time: 15 Minutes*

*Cook Time: 40 Minutes*

*Serves: 8*

This Cream Cheese Pound Cake is keto-friendly, low-carb, and incredibly tasty! Buttery, sweet, and creamy keto pound cake made with almond flour.

## Nutrition

Calories: 304kcal | Carbohydrates: 7g | Fiber: 2g | Sugar: 1g | Protein: 9g | Fat: 27g

## Ingredients

- 4 Eggs
- 4 ounces Cream Cheese, at room temperature
- 2 cups Superfine Almond Flour
- 2 teaspoons Baking Powder
- 4 tablespoons softened butter
- 1/2 cup Swerve, or Truvia
- 1 Teaspoon Almond Extract
- 1/4 cup sour cream

## Instructions

1. Preheat the oven to 350 degrees Fahrenheit. Set aside a 6-cup Bundt pan that has been greased. In a large stand-up mixer bowl, whip together the butter, cream cheese, and Swerve using the paddle attachment until light and fluffy and well combined.
2. Mix in the almond extract thoroughly.
3. Mix in the eggs and sour cream thoroughly.
4. Mix in all of the dry ingredients until everything is completely blended. Using an electric mixer, beat the ingredients until it is light and fluffy.
5. Pour the batter into a Bundt pan that has been oiled. Cook for 40 minutes, or until a toothpick inserted near the center comes out clean.
6. Cut up slices and freeze individual slices for a quick sweet hunger fix.
7. This recipe necessitates the use of almond flour.
8. Make sure the batter is fully mixed.
9. Instead of the huge 10-12 cup Bundt pan, use a six-cup Bundt pan.

# *KETO MINT BROWNIES*

*Prep Time: 15 Minutes*

*Chill Time: 15 Minutes*

*Serves: 12*

Mint and chocolate are a match made in heaven, and these Keto Mint Brownies are proof of that! They're minty, chocolaty, and low Carb at the same time.

**Nutrition**

Calories: 215kcal | Fat: 21g | Fiber: 2g | Carbohydrates: 6g | Protein: 3g

## Ingredients

<u>For the Base</u>

- 1 cup Superfine Almond Flour
- 1 cup Sugar-Free Chocolate Chips
- 1/2 cup butter

<u>For the Topping</u>

- 6 tablespoons Heavy Whipping Cream
- 1 teaspoon peppermint extract
- 1 drop of green food coloring
- 1/4 cup butter, softened
- 1/3 cup Powdered Swerve

## Instructions

1. Using shortening or cooking spray, lightly butter an 8 x 6-inch square pan.
2. In a large microwave-safe bowl, combine the butter and chocolate. Microwave for fifteen-twenty seconds, constantly stirring, until the butter and chocolate are completely melted. Mix in the almond flour thoroughly. Refrigerate this mixture after patting it into the oiled pan.
3. 1/4 cup butter, whipped cream, peppermint extract, and food color in a small bowl, whisk with an electric mixer on medium speed until completely combined. Gradually beat in powdered Swerve on low speed until smooth.
4. Using a spatula, evenly distribute the peppermint mixture over the chocolate mixture. Refrigerate for fifteen-twenty minutes before serving. Cut 5 rows by 5 rows for the bars. Green food coloring can be used in the frosting if desired.
5. If you microwave the chocolate for too long, it will start to solidify and spoil the recipe. Stirring is the ideal method for allowing the melted butter to finish melting the chocolate.

# **KETO PATRIOTIC DESSERT - CHEESECAKE MOUSSE**

*Prep Time:* 5 Minutes

*Cook Time:* 0 Minutes

*Serves:* 4

Looking for a patriotic Keto dessert? This two-ingredient cheesecake mousse is quick and easy to make, and it's excellent for any red, white, and blue event you're planning.

**Nutrition**

Calories: 433kcal | Protein: 2g | Fat: 44g | Carbohydrates: 8g

## Ingredients

- 5-6 drops blue gel food coloring
- 2 cups Heavy Whipping Cream
- 1 box sugar-free cheesecake instant pudding

<u>Optional Garnish</u>

- 4 slices Fresh Strawberries
- 4 teaspoons Unsweetened Shredded Coconut

## Instructions

1. In a large mixing bowl, combine the pudding and heavy whipping cream.
2. Mix the ingredients in a mixing bowl and whisk until thick peaks form.
3. Fold in the blue food coloring until no more streaks remain.
4. To serve, top each bowl with a spoonful of coconut and a strawberry slice. Chill before serving.
5. The optional coconut is not included in the macros.

# KETO BIG MAC SAUCE

*Prep Time: 5 Minutes*

*Cook Time: 5 Minutes*

*Serves: 6*

When you have the chance to eat nutritious, low-carb, and guilt-free sauce, who needs harmful, preservative-rich sauces?

**Nutrition**

Calories: 195kcal | Fiber: 1g | Fat: 21g | Sugar: 1g | Carbohydrates: 1g | Protein: 1g

## Ingredients

- 0.5 teaspoon Smoked Paprika
- 4 4 teaspoon Prepared Mustard
- 1 tablespoon onions, chopped
- 0.75 cup Mayonnaise
- 1 tablespoon White Vinegar
- 2 teaspoon Swerve

## Instructions

1. Combine all ingredients in a mixing bowl.
2. Serve with your favorite side dish.

# *DELICIOUS LOW CARB SCUFFINS - CARBQUIK*

*Prep Time: 10 Minutes*

*Cook Time: 20 Minutes*

*Serves: 12*

Make low-carb Scuffins with low sugar dried fruit and Carb quick, a hybrid between low-carb scones and low-carb muffins that will fulfill your sweet tooth. Light, moist, and delicious Scuffins

**Nutrition**

Calories: 151kcal | Fiber: 7g | Sugar: 7g | Carbohydrates: 8g | Fat: 10g | Protein: 3g

# Ingredients

## Mixed Fruit

- 1 cup Fresh Mixed Berries can be subbed for dried fruit
- 3/4 cup Dried Fruit, soaked for an hour

## Other Ingredients

- 1 Egg
- 1/4 cup butter
- 1/2 cup Heavy Whipping Cream
- 1 teaspoon Almond Extract
- 1/3 cup Truvia or other sweeteners
- 2 cups Carb quick baking mix

# Instructions

1. Soak one cup of mixed fruit in two cups of boiling water for thirty minutes with very little to no sugar added. Drain the water and replace it with fresh hot water for another thirty minutes. You're doing this to remove any extra sugar from the fruit as well as rehydrate the dried fruit.
2. Allow the fruit to drain for fifteen minutes using a filter.
3. This step can be skipped if you're using fresh fruit.
4. Preheat the oven to 375 degrees Fahrenheit.
5. While the fruit drains and the oven heat up, cut the butter into the Carbquik with a pastry cutter. Combine the egg, 1/2 cup heavy cream, almond essence, and sugar substitute in a separate bowl.
6. Add to the dry ingredients and stir until completely mixed.
7. In a large mixing bowl, add rehydrated mixed fruit and fresh berries. Make 12 balls with the dough and set them on a greased cookie sheet. Push down to flatten and neaten the edges slightly.
8. Bake for fifteen-twenty minutes at 375 degrees until the tops are browned, and a toothpick inserted in the center comes out clean.

# SPICY MAYO - KOREAN MAYONNAISE

*Prep Time: 5 Minutes*

*Cook Time: 0 Minutes*

*Serves: 4*

Do you want to boost the ante on your next burger or sandwich? Gochujang Mayonnaise is a must-try. This recipe is ridiculously easy to make and is quite spicy and tasty

**Nutrition**

Calories: 138kcal | Fiber: 1g | Sugar: 1g | Carbohydrates: 2g | Fat: 15g | Protein: 1g

## Ingredients

- 1/4 cup Chopped Green Scallions, chopped
- 1 tablespoon gochujang
- 2 teaspoon Sesame Seeds
- 1 tablespoon Sesame Oil
- 1/4 cup Mayonnaise

## Instructions

Combine the mayonnaise, gochujang, sesame oil, sesame seeds, and scallions in a mixing bowl.

# KETO BLACKBERRY COCONUT BAKE

*Prep Time: 10 Minutes*

*Cook Time: 20 Minutes*

*Serves: 6*

This Blackberry Coconut Bake is packed with blackberry flavor and really simple to prepare. And, best of all, it's dairy-free, low-carb, and low-sugar.

**Nutrition**

Calories: 65kcal | Fiber: 5g | Sugar: 4g | Carbohydrates: 7g | Fat: 1g | Protein: 2g

## Ingredients

- 1 Egg
- 1/2 teaspoon Xanthan Gum
- 2 tablespoons Truvia
- 1/4 cup coconut flour
- 1 Frozen Blackberry, thawed but not drained
- 1 teaspoon Baking Powder

## Instructions

1. Set aside a 7 x 2-inch cake pan that has been greased.
2. Add the berries, liquid, coconut flour, egg, Truvia, baking powder, and xanthan gum in a medium mixing bowl.
3. Pour into a prepared baking sheet and bake for twenty minutes at 350°F. Allow ten minutes for the pudding to cool before serving hot. Whipped cream or keto ice cream can be added to the top.
4. This delicacy is best served either steaming hot when it has a softer, pudding-like consistency and can be scooped, or cold when it keeps its shape when cut into slices.

# PUMPKIN CHEESECAKE MOUSSE

*Prep Time: 10 Minutes*

*Chill Time: 60 Minutes*

*Serves: 8*

This Pumpkin Cheesecake Mousse is a delicious way to satisfy your pumpkin dessert cravings without the added sugar or fat. Plus, it's a cinch to make.

**Nutrition**

Calories: 215kcal | Fiber: 1g | Sugar: 3g | Carbohydrates: 8g | Fat: 19g | Protein: 3g

## Ingredients

- 2 scoops Syntax Vanilla Bean protein powder 2 cups Whole Milk
- 2 packages sugar-free cheesecake instant pudding
- 2 teaspoons Pumpkin Pie Spice
- 1 can pumpkin puree
- 1.5 cup heavy whipping cream (Optional)

## Instructions

1. Combine the pudding mix, milk, pumpkin, protein powder (if using), and pumpkin pie spice in a blender and blend until smooth, about 1-2 minutes. Set aside.
2. Using a hand-held mixer or the bowl of your Kitchen aid mixer, whip the heavy cream until stiff.
3. In a mixing dish, gently stir the whipped cream into the pumpkin cheesecake pudding until fully combined.
4. Allow it to chill for a few hours before serving.
5. If you mix this mousse with oatmeal or overnight oats, it becomes even more wonderful
6. You can omit the vanilla protein powder if you don't have any on hand.

# HIGH PROTEIN JELLO MOUSSE

*Prep Time: 5 Minutes*

*Cook Time: 20 Minutes*

*Serves: 4*

The sugar-free Jello, Greek yogurt, and plain protein powder in this high-protein Jello mousse provide a great protein punch.

**Nutrition**

Calories: 42kcal | Fat: 1g | Sugar: 2g | Protein: 7g | Carbohydrates: 3g

## Ingredients

- 1 cup Water
- 1 scoop NOW unflavored whey
- 1 small box sugar-free Black Cherry Jello
- 10 oz Full-Fat Greek Yogurt

## Instructions

1. Warm the water, but not to the point of boiling it.
2. Empty the sugar-free Jello mix into a mixing bowl, pour the water over it, and set it aside while you organize the other ingredients.
3. Now I'll use my regular sophisticated cooking method to throw everything into the mixing bowl. Blend until completely smooth.
4. Pour into four ramekins and put them aside to cool.
5. When making this dish, the essential thing to remember is to be patient and ensure that the gelatin is thoroughly dissolved in the water before you begin. If you don't do this, your mousse will have granules, which is not good.
6. To aerate this mousse as much as possible, use a flat silicone whisk or a hand blender.
7. To make different desserts, mix up the flavors.

# KETO CHOCOLATE CHAFFLES

*Prep Time: 10 Minutes*

*Cook Time: 10 Minutes*

*Serves: 2*

Keto Chocolate Chaffles are quite simple to prepare. This delectable 5-ingredient keto waffle recipe is nut-free, keto-friendly, low-carb, vegetarian, and, most importantly, tasty.

**Nutrition**

Calories: 672kcal | Carbohydrates: 7g | Fiber: 5g | Fat: 70g | Sugar: 1g | Protein: 13g

## Ingredients

- 3 Eggs
- 1/2 cup Sugar-Free Chocolate Chips
- 1/4 cup Truvia or other sweeteners
- 1 teaspoon Vanilla extract
- 1/2 cup butter

## Instructions

1. Melt butter and chocolate in a microwave-safe bowl for about one minute. Remove the lid and give it a good swirl. The heat from the butter and chocolate is used to melt the remaining clumps. You've overcooked the chocolate if you microwave it until it's completely melted. So, grab a spoon and get to work. If necessary, add another ten seconds, but stir thoroughly first.
2. In a mixing bowl, whisk together the eggs, sweetener, and vanilla extract until light and fluffy.
3. In a gentle stream, pour the melted butter and chocolate into the mixing bowl and beat until fully combined.
4. Cook for seven-eight minutes, or until crispy, in a Dash Mini Waffle Maker with roughly 1/4 of the ingredients.
5. There should be enough batter left over to create 4 waffles.
6. To get the finest results, serve these warm with whipped cream or syrup.
7. If you microwave the chocolate too long, it will burn. Cook and stir until the mixture is smooth and melted.
8. These are great for freezing! Make a large quantity and freeze some of it to reheat later.

# RASPBERRY CREAM BOMBS

*Prep Time: 10 Minutes*

*Cook Time: 10 Minutes*

*Serves: 6*

Raspberry Cream Bombs are a delicious low-carb keto dessert! They don't require any cooking, are really simple to prepare and are absolutely delicious.

**Nutrition**

Calories: 198kcal | Fat: 20g | Sugar: 1g | Carbohydrates: 2g | Protein: 2g

## Ingredients

- 1/2 cup Heavy Whipping Cream
- 8 ounces Cream Cheese
- 1/2 cup hot water
- 1 small package sugar-free Raspberry Jello

## Instructions

1. Fill the stand mixer bowl halfway with boiling water.
2. Sprinkle Jello on top and set aside for a few minutes to soften. Stir everything together thoroughly. If there are still Jello crystals in there, add a bit more boiling water and stir until they dissolve.
3. Slowly begin to beat the mixture with a whisk attachment, adding cream cheese and heavy whipping cream as needed.

# KETO MILKY CHOCOLATE TRUFFLES

*Prep Time: 5 Minutes*

*Cook Time: 5 Minutes*

*Serves: 6*

These low-carb Keto Truffles are deliciously sweet, milky, and low in carbs! They're also very simple to make with only three ingredients

**Nutrition**

Calories: 106kcal | Fat: 11g | Fiber: 1g | Carbohydrates: 3g | Protein: 1g

## Ingredients

- 1 tablespoon butter
- 1/4 cup Heavy Whipping Cream
- 1/2 cup Sugar-Free Chocolate Chips

## Instructions

1. Grease a small 12-cup truffle mold with 1 teaspoon of butter in each cavity. In a heatproof cup with a pouring lip, combine all of the ingredients. The quickest way to achieve this is to use coconut oil Pam spray.
2. Microwave for thirty seconds. Remove the lid and give it a good swirl. Instead of overcooking this mixture, let all of the components melt in the residual heat. If there are chunks of un-melted butter or chocolate after vigorous swirling for thirty seconds, return it to the microwave in ten-second increments, stirring between cook cycles.
3. Fill a tiny 12-cavity truffle mold halfway with the mixture. Freeze the truffles for thirty minutes before unmolding and an hour after they've set. Remove from the oven and place in a covered container in the refrigerator. Each dish yields two tiny truffles.

# *INSTANT POT THAI COCONUT PANDAN CUSTARD*

*Prep Time: 5 Minutes*

*Cook Time: 30 Minutes*

*Serves: 4*

Thai Coconut Pandan Custard is a delightful Keto, and Low Carb dessert made entirely in your Instant Pot.

**Nutrition**

Calories: 174kcal | Fat: 14g | Carbohydrates: 6g | Protein: 6g

## Ingredients

- 3 Eggs
- 1/3 cup Truvia
- 1 cup Full-Fat Coconut Milk
- 3-4 drops Pandan Extract

## Instructions

1. Combine the eggs, milk, sweetener, and Pandan essence in a 6-inch heatproof bowl and whisk until smooth. Wrap foil around the dish.
2. Fill your liner with 2 cups of water, add a trivet, and set your bowl on top of the trivet.
3. Cook for thirty minutes on high pressure, then naturally release the pressure. A knife should come out clean when inserted into the custard.

# MEXICAN HOT CHOCOLATE MIX

*Prep Time: 10 Minutes*

*Cook Time: 2 Minutes*

*Serves: 8*

This Mexican Hot Chocolate Mix produces a delicious cup of hot chocolate with a Mexican flair! It's sweet and spicy with just the proper amount of spiciness

**Nutrition**

Calories: 102kcal | Fiber: 2g | Sugar: 6g | Fat: 5g | Carbohydrates: 8g | Protein: 5g

## Ingredients

- 1/2 cup Unsweetened Cocoa Powder
- 1 cup Whole Milk Powder
- 1 tablespoon Ground Cinnamon
- 1 teaspoon Ancho Chile Powder
- 2 tablespoons Cornstarch
- 1/2 cup Truvia

## Instructions

1. Using a whisk, combine all of the ingredients. That's all there is to it.
2. Place 2-3 tablespoons of the mix in a cup, add boiling water, and microwave for thirty seconds when ready to use. Stir vigorously to allow the sauce to thicken.
3. Microwave for one-two minutes, stirring every thirty seconds if using tap water.

# STEVIA SWEETENED BLUEBERRY FRUIT LEATHER

*Prep Time: 20 Minutes*

*Cook Time: 120 Minutes*

*Serves: 12*

Fruit rolls are a terrific technique to keep fruit fresh for a long time. The majority of store-bought fruit leathers have additional sugar or fruit juice. Low-carb stevia is used to sweeten these handmade versions.

**Nutrition**

Calories: 23 | Carbohydrates: 7g | Fat:0g | Protein: 0g | Fiber: 1g | Sugar: 5g

Cholesterol: 0mg

## Ingredients

- ½ teaspoon stevia glycerite
- 4 cups blueberries, fresh or frozen

## Instructions

1. In a food processor, combine blueberries and stevia. Puree until the mixture is completely smooth. Fill the center of Teflex or plastic wrap-covered food dehydrator trays with 1 1/2 to 2 cups puree. Place puree on a tray and spread it out. Because the puree dries faster at the edges, it should be spread about 18 inches thick in the center and 1/4 inches thick at the edges.
2. Placed the prepared trays in a food dehydrator set to 135 degrees Fahrenheit. The drying time ranges from four to six hours on average. When the leather has dried, it will be a little shinier and less sticky. Allow the leather to cool completely before removing it from the tray. Make strips out of it. Wrap strips in waxed paper and keep them in an airtight container.

# *LOW CARB KETO STRAWBERRY SHORTCAKE*

*Prep Time: 15 Minutes*

*Cook Time: 55 Minutes*

*Serves: 16*

Make a delicious low-carb almond flour pound cake. Simply top with fresh strawberries and whipped cream for a delicious gluten-free strawberry shortcake.

**Nutrition**

Calories: 224 | Carbohydrates: 6g | Protein: 6g | Fat: 20g | Fiber: 2g | Sugar: 1g

Saturated Fat: 6g | Cholesterol: 74mg

## Ingredients

### For Low Carb Pound Cake

- 1 ½ cups plus 2 tablespoons almond flour
- ½ cup powdered erythritol or Swerve
- ¼ teaspoon stevia concentrated powder
- 4 ounces cream cheese softened
- ½ cup butter softened
- 1 teaspoon lemon extract
- 5 eggs room temperature
- 1 teaspoon baking powder
- 1 teaspoon vanilla extract

### For Strawberry Shortcake

- sugar-free whipped cream
- 16 strawberries
- Instructions

## Instructions

### For Pound Cake

1. Using an electric mixer, whip together the butter, cream cheese, erythritol, and stevia. Blend in the extracts one at a time as you add the eggs one at a time.
2. Combine the almond flour and baking powder; gradually add to the egg mixture.
3. Pour into a 9-inch loaf pan that has been oiled and baked at 325°F for fifty-fifty five minutes, or until thoroughly browned.
4. Allow it to cool for ten minutes before removing it from the pan.

### For Strawberry Shortcake

1. Cut two pieces of pound cake in half.
2. Slice two strawberries.
3. Top the bottom cake with one sliced strawberry and sugar-free whipped cream.
4. Repeat for the upper layer.

# MATCHA GREEN TEA CHIA PUDDING

*Prep Time: 15 Minutes*

*Cook Time: 0 Minutes*

*Serves: 6*

Matcha, green tea, and chia seeds are all recognized to have numerous health benefits. This tasty low-carb matcha green tea chia pudding will give you a health boost.

## Nutrition

Calories: 182 | Carbohydrates: 4.2g | Sodium: 2mg | Fiber: 14.9g | Protein: 8.6g

Fat: 14.9g | Saturated Fat: 0.9g

## Ingredients

- ⅓ cup chia seeds
- ¼ cup low carb sugar substitute
- 4 bags matcha green tea
- 1 ¾ cup unsweetened almond milk or coconut milk
- ⅓ cup boiling water

## Instructions

1. Green tea should be steeped in water for three-five minutes. Bags must be removed.
2. To brewed tea, add sugar, almond milk, and chia seeds. Stir everything together thoroughly.
3. Stir every five minutes for the next fifteen minutes.
4. If desired, divide into serving dishes. Refrigerate until completely set.

# HOMEMADE BUTTERSCOTCH PUDDING

*Prep Time: 5 Minutes*

*Cook Time: 15 Minutes*

*Serves: 12*

This low-carb butterscotch pudding will fill you up even if you just eat a tiny bit. It incorporates regular butter and a brown sugar replacement.

**Nutrition**

Calories: 197 | Carbohydrates: 3.9g | Fiber: 1.5g | Sugar: 2.3g | Cholesterol: 78mg

Protein: 2.5g | Fat: 20.3g

## Ingredients

- 4 egg yolks
- 2 cans coconut cream 13.5 ounces each or use about 3 ⅓ cups heavy cream
- ½ cup Sukrin Gold or your favorite low carb brown sugar replacement
- ½ teaspoon xanthan gum or guar gum, adjust to get desired thickness
- 1 teaspoon Sweet Leaf stevia drops
- ¼ teaspoon sea salt
- 3 tablespoons butter
- 1 tablespoon vanilla extract
- ⅛ teaspoon nutmeg

## Instructions

1. Combine Sukrin Gold, salt, and coconut cream in a big saucepan.
2. Cook, constantly stirring, until the mixture boils.
3. Reduce heat to low and continue to simmer and stir for another two minutes.
4. Remove the pan from the heat.
5. Return all to the pan after slowly stirring in approximately 1/2 cup of the hot mixture into the egg yolks.
6. Bring to a slow boil, continually stirring.
7. Cook for another 2 minutes, or until the mixture has thickened.
8. Remove the pan from the heat.
9. Combine the stevia liquid, butter, nutmeg, and vanilla extract in a mixing bowl.
10. Xanthan gum is a thickening agent pudding that will thicken a lot after cooling in the refrigerator.
11. Allow for fifteen minutes of cooling time, stirring occasionally.
12. Into a large mixing bowl or individual serving cups, transfer the mixture.
13. Cover and chill until ready to serve. If desired, top with whipped cream.

# GLUTEN-FREE TIRAMISU WHOOPIE PIES – LOW CARB

*Prep Time: 23 Minutes*

*Cook Time: 12 Minutes*

*Serves: 12*

Mini low-carb tiramisu whoopie pies to help you get through the day. A creamy filling spiced with espresso and rum fills the gluten-free cookies.

**Nutrition**

Calories: 344 | Carbohydrates: 8g | Protein: 10g | Fat: 32g | Cholesterol: 91mg

Fiber: 2g | Sugar: 1g

# Ingredients

## Cookies

- 2 large eggs
- ½ cup low carb sugar substitute or ½ cup of your favorite low carb sweetener
- ½ cup Lakanto Golden Monk Fruit Granular Sweetener
- 3 tablespoons unflavored whey protein
- 2 teaspoons baking powder
- ½ cup butter cut into small cubes
- 2 cups almond flour
- ½ teaspoon baking soda
- 1 teaspoon vanilla extract
- ½ cup full-fat sour cream
- cocoa powder for dusting
- ½ teaspoon salt

## Filling

- ½ cup heavy cream
- 2 teaspoons vanilla extract
- ¼ cup cold espresso coffee or strong coffee
- 2 tablespoon low carb sugar substitute
- 8-ounce mascarpone cheese
- 2 teaspoons dark rum optional
- 1 tablespoon dark rum optional
- pinch of salt

# Instructions

1. Preheat the oven to 350 degrees Fahrenheit. Coat a whoopie pie pan in nonstick cooking spray.
2. In a large mixing bowl, combine almond flour, protein powder, brown sugar sweetener, baking powder, baking soda, and salt. Set aside
3. On medium-high speed, beat butter and sugar until creamy, about two minutes. Beat in the eggs and 1 teaspoon vanilla extract until fully combined. Scrape the bowl's sides clean.
4. Scoop the batter into each whoopie pie shape with a tiny teaspoon, filling about 2/3 of the way. In a tiny colander, place some cocoa powder and sprinkle a little on top of each batter scoop.

5. Bake for ten-twelve minutes, or until brown around the edges.
6. Cool for ten minutes on a wire rack before removing cookies from the pan and allowing them to cool completely. Cookies that haven't been filled can be kept for up to a day.
7. Turn cookies upside-down on the rack once they've cooled.
8. In a small dish, combine espresso and 3 tablespoons of black rum. On the bottom side of each biscuit, spread roughly a quarter teaspoon of espresso liquid.
9. With a mixer, beat together mascarpone cheese, low carb sugar alternative, salt, heavy cream vanilla, and 1 tablespoon dark rum until smooth. Place a spoonful of the mascarpone cheese mixture on the chocolate half of the cookies. Place the remaining half of the cookies on top of that. Serve right away or store in the refrigerator. These cookies can also be frozen after being individually wrapped in plastic.

# *EASY DOUBLE CHOCOLATE CHAFFLES*

*Prep Time: 1 Minute*

*Cook Time: 4 Minutes*

*Serves: 1*

Breakfast or dessert, double chocolate chaffles are delicious. Recipes for delicious, easy, and amusing chaffles that the whole family will enjoy.

**Nutrition**

Calories: 337.7 | Net Carbohydrates: 6.5g | Fiber: 4.8g | Sugar: 2g | Protein: 24.3g

Total Carbohydrates: 11.3g

## Ingredients

<u>Double Chocolate Chaffles</u>

- 1 egg - medium
- 1 tablespoon granulated sweetener of choice or more to your taste
- 1 tablespoon sugar-free chocolate chips or cacao nibs
- ½ cup pre-shredded/grated mozzarella
- 2 tablespoon almond meal/flour
- 2 tablespoon cocoa powder unsweetened
- 1 teaspoon heavy/double cream
- 1 teaspoon vanilla

## Instructions

1. In a mixing bowl, combine the ingredients for your preferred flavor.
2. Preheat the waffle iron. Spray the mini-waffle maker with olive oil once it's hot, and pour half the batter into it or the entire batter into a large waffle maker.
3. Cook for two-four minutes before removing and repeating the process. Per recipe, you should be able to produce 2 mini-chaffles or 1 giant chaffle.
4. Garnish, serve, and savor.

# KETO CHAFFLE GARLIC CHEESY BREAD STICKS

*Prep Time: 3 Minutes*

*Cook Time: 7 Minutes*

*Serves: 8*

A simple keto recipe for low-carb, gluten-free breadstick appetizers or desserts.

**Nutrition**

Calories: 74kcal | Fat: 6.5g | Fiber: 0.2g | Carbohydrates: 0.9g | Protein: 3.4g

## Ingredients

- ½ cup mozzarella cheese grated
- 2 tablespoons almond flour
- ½ teaspoon garlic powder
- ½ teaspoon oregano
- ½ teaspoon salt
- 1 medium egg

Topping

- 2 tablespoons butter, unsalted softened
- ¼ cup mozzarella cheese grated
- ½ teaspoon garlic powder

## Instructions

1. Lightly oil your waffle maker before using it.
2. Beat the egg in a mixing bowl.
3. Mix in the mozzarella, almond flour, garlic powder, oregano, and salt until thoroughly combined.
4. Fill your waffle maker halfway with batter. If using a smaller waffle machine, spoon in half of the ingredients at a time. This combination covers both waffle areas on my square double waffle.
5. Lightly oil your waffle maker before using it.
6. Beat the egg in a mixing bowl.
7. Mix in the mozzarella, almond flour, garlic powder, oregano, and salt until thoroughly combined.
8. Fill your waffle maker halfway with batter. If using a smaller waffle machine, spoon in half of the ingredients at a time.
9. Spoon the batter into the waffle maker's center and gently spread it out to the edges.
10. Cook for five minutes with the lid closed.
11. Remove the cooked waffles with tongs and cut each waffle into four sections.
12. Preheat the grill and arrange the sticks on a tray.
13. Combine the butter and garlic powder, then sprinkle it over the sticks.
14. Place the mozzarella sticks under the grill for two to three minutes or until the cheese has melted and is bubbling. Eat right away

# *LOW-CARB DARK CHERRY CRUNCH PIE*

*Prep Time: 15 Minutes*

*Cook Time: 25 Minutes*

*Serves: 8*

This pie is perfect for people who have food allergies. It's grain-free and sugar-free, as are all of my recipes. In addition, this pie is dairy-free and egg-free. To make it nut-free, substitute the nuts with extra coconut and use crushed sunflower seeds instead of almond flour.

**Nutrition**

Calories: 335kcal | Net Carbohydrates: 6.7g | Fiber: 6.7g | Sugar: 5.8g | Fat28.8g

Saturated Fat: 12.3g | Protein: 8.2g

## Ingredients

<u>Crust</u>

- 3 tablespoons extra virgin coconut oil, melted
- 1/2 cup pecan nuts, coarsely chopped 1 cup desiccated coconut
- 1/4 cup powdered Erythritol or Swerve
- 10-15 drops liquid Stevia extract
- 1 cup almond flour

<u>Topping</u>

- 1 tablespoon extra-virgin coconut oil, melted
- 1 1/2 cups Dark Cherry Chia Jam
- 1 cup almonds, flaked
- 5-10 drops liquid Stevia extract
- 1 tablespoon Erythritol or Swerve
- 1 cup dried coconut, flaked
- pinch of sea salt

## Instructions

1. Preheat the oven to 175 degrees Celsius/ 350 degrees Fahrenheit or 195 degrees Celsius/ 380 degrees Fahrenheit. Chop the pecan nuts coarsely and combine them with desiccated coconut, almond flour, and heated coconut oil in a mixing bowl. Mix in the erythritol and stevia well.
2. To make the edges, press the mixture into a tart baking dish and use your fingers to make them. Preheat oven to 350°F and bake for twelve-fifteen minutes. To avoid burning, keep an eye on it.
3. Remove the pan from the oven and lay it on a rack to cool before filling with Dark Cherry Chia Jam.
4. Using a spatula, spread the jam all over the pie.
5. Combine the flaked almonds, coconut flakes, and melted coconut oil in a small bowl. Erythritol, stevia, and salt are added.
6. Sprinkle equally over the top of the pie and bake for an additional seven to ten minutes.
7. Place the pie on a cooling rack and set it aside to cool completely before serving.

# KETO GOLDEN MILK ICE CREAM

*Prep Time: 10 Minutes*

*Chill Time: 6 Hours*

*Serves: 4*

Ice cream is made with only four ingredients and flavored with coconut and turmeric.

**Nutrition**

Calories: 351kcal | Sugar: 2 | Fiber: 1 | Protein: 2 | Carbohydrates: 5 | Fat: 37

## Ingredients

- 2 cans of full-fat unsweetened coconut milk, room temperature
- 1/3 cup of erythritol or sweetener of choice
- 2 teaspoons of vanilla extract
- 1 tablespoon of turmeric
- Dash of salt

## Instructions

1. In a blender, add all of the ingredients and blend for three minutes.
2. Fill an ice cream maker halfway with the mixture and churn according to the manufacturer's directions. Place the ice cream in a freezer-safe container once it has been churned and frozen until ready to serve.
3. If you don't have an ice cream machine, transfer the mixture to a freezer-safe container and freeze it. Allow the ice cream to freeze entirely, about four hours, after stirring every thirty minutes for the first two to three hours.
4. To serve, take the container out of the freezer and set it aside for ten minutes to get to room temperature before scooping and serving.

# KETO MIXED BERRY CRUMBLE

*Prep Time: 10 Minutes*

*Cook Time: 25 Minutes*

*Serves: 6*

This is the ideal dessert for a hot summer day.

**Nutrition**

Calories: 198kcal | Sugar: 4g | Fat: 17g | Fiber: 5g | Protein: 2g | Carbohydrates: 6g

**Ingredients**

- 1/2 cup of almond flour
- 3 tablespoons of coconut oil, solid
- 3/4 cup of shredded coconut
- 1 cup of mixed berries
- 1/2 teaspoon of vanilla extract
- 1 tablespoon of lemon juice

**Instructions**

1. Preheat the oven to 350°F.
2. Combine the berries and lemon juice in a bowl, gently squishing the berries as you combine. Divide the berries between 6 shallow ovenproof dishes on a try or one ovenproof dish. Bake for fifteen minutes
3. Cut the firm coconut oil into small pieces while the berries are baking. In a mixing dish, combine the almond flour and coconut oil bits. Mix in the vanilla and crushed coconut until it resembles breadcrumbs.
4. Remove the berries from the oven and sprinkle the crumb mixture evenly over the top.

# *KETO MINI PECAN PIES*

*Prep Time: 15 Minutes*

*Cook Time: 15 Minutes*

*Serves: 6*

This recipe for keto little pecan pies can only be described in one word: gorgeous. To satiate your sweet taste, make them as a special treat.

**Nutrition**

Calories: 243kcal | Sugar: 1g | Fat: 24g | Protein: 6g | Fiber: 3g | Carbohydrates: 4g

## Ingredients

### For the crust

- 1/2 cup (60 g) almond flour
- 2 tablespoons erythritol or stevia
- 2 tablespoons flax meal
- 2 tablespoon ghee
- 1 egg, whisked

### For the filling

- 1 egg, whisked
- 1/4 cup erythritol or stevia
- 1/2 cup pecans, chopped
- 1 teaspoon vanilla extract
- 1/4 cup ghee

## Instructions

1. Preheat the oven to 350 degrees Fahrenheit (175 C).
2. To make the crust, combine all of the crust ingredients in a mixing bowl. To make the crust, press the dough into 6 small muffin cups.
3. In a large mixing bowl, combine all of the filling ingredients.
4. Pour the mixture into the six crusts.
5. Bake for fifteen minutes, or until the crust is golden brown.
6. Allow it to cool before eating.

# WORLD'S GREATEST LOW CARB KETO WAFFLES

*Prep Time: 5 Minutes*

*Cook Time: 3 Minutes*

*Serves: 1*

That's it. The Best Low-Carb Pancake and Waffle Batter on the Planet. Without a doubt.

**Nutrition**

Calories: 522kcal | Fat: 48g | Fiber: 2g | Protein: 19g | Carbohydrates: 7g

**Ingredients**

- 1 tablespoon coconut oil or melted butter
- 2 – 4 tablespoons almond flour
- 1/2 teaspoon baking powder
- 2 oz cream cheese
- 2 large eggs

**Instructions**

1. In a blender, combine all of the ingredients and blend until smooth.
2. Pour the batter into a waffle maker that has been preheated and lightly greased, and bake according to the manufacturer's instructions. It usually takes about two to three minutes.
3. Lift it off the grid with a fork once it's finished.

# *LOW CARB SEMIFREDDO*

*Prep Time: 10 Minutes*

*Cook Time: 10 Minutes*

*Chill Time: 6 Hours*

*Serves: 10*

This low-carb semifreddo is made with almonds and chocolate chips and is served frozen.

**Nutrition**

Calories: 194kcal | Total Fat: 17g | Cholesterol: 101mg | Carbohydrates: 10g

Fiber: 4g | Protein: 5g | Net Carbohydrates: 6g

## Ingredients

- 3 whole eggs
- 1 cup heavy cream
- ¾ cup low carb sweetener, e.g. Lakanto
- ¾ cup almond flour
- ½ cup low carb dark chocolate chips, approx. 3 oz
- 1 teaspoon vanilla extract
- 1 egg yolk
- 2 tablespoons brandy, optional
- toasted sliced almonds to garnish

## Instructions

1. In a mixing dish, lightly whisk together the eggs and sweetener. Cook the mixture over a saucepan of boiling water to produce a bain-marie until the sweetener has dissolved and the temperature is comfortable.
2. Remove from the fire and stir in the almond flour and, if using, the brandy. Allow it to cool before serving.
3. In a stand mixer dish, whisk together the heavy cream and vanilla extract until soft peaks form. Combine the chilled egg mixture and chocolate chips in a mixing bowl.
4. Pour the ingredients into a loaf pan that has been lined with plastic wrap. Place for at least six hours or overnight in the freezer.
5. Remove it from the freezer five minutes before serving and remove it out of the pan with the plastic wrap, flipping it over onto a baking tray. Serve with toasted sliced almonds as a garnish. Serve immediately after cutting into slices.

# KETO CANNOLI CHEESECAKE

*Prep Time: 15 Minutes*

*Chill Time: 4-6 Hours*

*Serves: 12*

With a light, creamy filling, Keto Cannoli cheesecake is sinfully wonderful. It's ideal for all-year entertaining and serving as a simple dessert. Cinnamon and chocolate are classic tastes in this cheesecake, and it only takes 9 ingredients and 15 minutes to prepare.

## Nutrition

Calories: 376kcal | Carbohydrates: 9g | Protein: 11g | Fiber: 3g | Sugar: 1g

Cholesterol: 70mg | Fat: 35g | Saturated Fat: 17g

## Ingredients

<u>Crust</u>

- 3 tablespoon almond butter
- 1 ½ cups almond flour
- ¼ cup Joy Filled Eats Sweetener
- ⅓ cup salted butter melted

<u>Filling</u>

- ½ cup Joy Filled Eats Sweetener
- 2 cups whole milk ricotta cheese
- 8 oz heavy whipping cream
- 4 oz cream cheese softened
- 1 cup sugar-free chocolate chips
- 2 teaspoons cinnamon
- 2 teaspoons gelatin
- ½ teaspoon vanilla

## Instructions

1. To make the crust, whisk together all of the ingredients until smooth. Make sure the almond butter is well incorporated. In a 9-inch springform pan, press the mixture into the bottom.
2. Bloom the gelatin. Sprinkle the gelatin on top of 2 tablespoons cold water Allow for five minutes of resting time. 2 tablespoons hot water, stirred in until dissolved
3. In a separate dish, whip the cream with an electric mixer until stiff peaks form.
4. 1/3 of the whipped cream must be folded into the cheesecake batter. Fold in the remaining ingredients gently. Combine the chocolate chips and fold them in. Pour over the crust that has been prepared.
5. Refrigerate for at least four-six hours or until it has firmed up. It keeps its softness like a mousse.

# *KETO DALGONA COFFEE – WHIPPED COFFEE*

*Prep Time: 3 Minutes*

*Cook Time: 0 Minutes*

*Serves: 4*

This three-ingredient keto Dalgona coffee may become your go-to beverage for weeks. It's very simple and wonderful

## Nutrition

Calories: 9kcal | Saturated Fat: 1g | Sodium: 1mg | Protein: 1g | Fat: 1g

Carbohydrates: 2g | Potassium: 88mg

## Ingredients

- 2 tablespoons boiling water
- 2 tablespoons sweetener
- 2 tablespoons instant coffee instant or granulated

To Serve

- 1 gallon of Keto Milk (click link for recipe) Choose your favorite dairy-free milk

## Instructions

Conventional Method

1. In a small but deep bowl, combine all of the ingredients. Whip the mixture with a hand mixer or a whisk until it is thick and pale. It just took me 2.5 minutes to get a thick mix with my hand mixer.

Thermomix Method

2. Note: Double the recipe if using the Thermomix
3. Insert Butterfly. Place all ingredients into a mixer bowl. Mix 3 min/speed 4.

# *LOW CARB ITALIAN CREAM CAKE*

*Prep Time: 45 Minutes*

*Cook Time: 45 Minutes*

*Serves: 16*

The low-carb and keto-friendly version of the classic Italian cream cake! This decadent layer cake is a one-of-a-kind delicacy that's well worth the effort.

**Nutrition**

Calories: 335kcal | Fat: 30.1g | Fiber: 2.4g | Protein: 5.8g | Carbohydrates: 5.7g

## Ingredients

### Cake

- 4 large eggs room temperature, separated
- 1/2 cup heavy cream room temperature
- 1/2 cup shredded coconut
- 1 cup Swerve Sweetener
- 1 1/2 cups almond flour
- 1/2 cup butter softened
- 1/2 cup chopped pecans
- 1 teaspoon vanilla extract
- 1/4 cup coconut flour
- 2 teaspoon baking powder
- 1/4 teaspoon cream of tartar
- 1/2 teaspoon salt

### Frosting

- 1 cup powdered Swerve Sweetener
- 8 ounces cream cheese softened
- 1/2 cup butter softened
- 1/2 cup heavy whipping cream room temperature
- 1 teaspoon vanilla extract

### Garnish

- 2 tablespoons chopped pecans lightly toasted
- 2 tablespoons shredded coconut lightly toasted

## Instructions

### Cake

1. Preheat the oven to 325°F and lightly butter two 8- or 9-inch round cake pans (the 8-inch pans will take a little longer to cook, but the layers will be higher, and I think they will look better). Grease the parchment paper and line the pans with it.
2. In a large mixing bowl, cream together the butter and sweetener until smooth. One at a time, beat in the egg yolks, incorporating well after each addition. Combine the heavy cream and vanilla extract in a mixing bowl.

3. Combine the almond flour, shredded coconut, chopped nuts, coconut flour, baking powder, and salt in a separate bowl. Incorporate the flour mixture into the butter mixture until it is completely mixed.
4. In a separate large mixing bowl, whisk the egg whites with the cream of tartar until stiff peaks form. Fold gently into the cake batter.
5. Spread the batter evenly between the prepared pans and around the borders. Bake for thirty-five to forty-five minutes or longer, depending on your pans, or until brown on the edges and firm to the touch in the center.
6. Remove from the oven and cool entirely in the pans before transferring to a wire rack to cool completely. If the parchment comes out with the layers, remove it.

Frosting

1. Cream together the cream cheese and butter in a large mixing bowl until smooth. Combine the sweetener and vanilla extract in a bowl and mix.
2. Slowly drizzle in the heavy whipping cream until it reaches a spreadable consistency.

To Assemble

1. Place the bottom layer on a serving plate and spread about a third of the frosting on top. Next, frost the top and sides of the next layer.
2. Toasted coconut and pecans will be sprinkled on top. Refrigerate for at least half an hour to allow the flavors to meld.

# **KETO BROWNIE MUFFINS**

*Prep Time: 15 Minutes*

*Cook Time: 20 Minutes*

*Serves: 8*

These brownie muffins are guaranteed to be a hit when shared. They're absolutely tasty.

**Nutrition**

Calories: 290kcal | Sugar: 1g | Fat: 26g | Carbohydrates: 9g | Net Carbohydrates: 4g

Protein: 8g | Fiber: 5

## Ingredients

- 3 large eggs, whisked
- 6 tablespoons coconut oil, melted
- 3 tablespoons chia seeds, ground
- 1 teaspoon vanilla extract
- 2 tablespoons almond milk
- 1/4 cup coconut cream
- 2 teaspoons baking powder
- 1/2 cup walnuts, chopped small
- 1/2 cup unsweetened cacao powder
- 1/2 cup erythritol + stevia, to taste
- 1 cup almond flour

## Instructions

1. Preheat the oven to 350 degrees Fahrenheit (175 C).
2. Melt the coconut oil in a small bowl and leave it aside to cool.
3. Combine the eggs, vanilla extract, coconut cream, and almond milk in a large mixing bowl. Combine the almond flour, baking powder, ground chia, erythritol, and cacao powder in a separate bowl. Add the walnuts, chopped.
4. When the coconut oil is cool enough to handle, whisk it into the egg mixture before adding it to the almond flour mixture. Combine the ingredients in a large mixing bowl and distribute evenly amongst 8 muffin tins sprayed with cooking spray.
5. Preheat the oven to 350°F and bake for fifteen-twenty minutes, or until a cake tester inserted in the center comes out clean.
6. Allow it to cool for a few minutes before carefully removing them with a sharp knife.

# *KETO GRAHAM CRACKERS*

*Prep Time: 10 Minutes*

*Cook Time: 10 Minutes*

*Serves: 8*

Keto graham crackers are delicious and simple to prepare. All you have to do is swap out the wheat, sugar, and fats in typical graham crackers for keto-friendly alternatives.

**Nutrition**

Calories: 199kcal | Sugar: 1g | Fat: 18g | Carbohydrates: 6g | Net Carbohydrates: 2g

Protein: 6g | Fiber: 4g

## Ingredients

- 1 large egg, whisked
- 2 cups almond flour
- 1 teaspoon baking powder
- 1/2 tablespoon cinnamon powder
- 3 tablespoons ghee, melted
- 2 tablespoons flax meal
- 1/4 cup erythritol
- Dash of salt

## Instructions

1. Preheat the oven to 350 degrees Fahrenheit (175 C).
2. To make a dough, combine all of the ingredients thoroughly.
3. Roll out the dough on parchment paper until it is as thin as possible. Cut the dough into 2 by 2-inch squares using a sharp knife or pizza cutter. Decorate by poking a few holes in the tops of each with a fork.
4. Place the parchment paper on a baking tray and bake for eight-ten minutes, or until the edges are just beginning to brown.
5. This recipe makes approximately 24 crackers.
6. In a graham cracker s'mores sandwich, add some Keto marshmallows and chocolate.

# KETO CHOCOLATE DIPPED STRAWBERRIES

*Prep Time: 5 Minutes*

*Cook Time: 5 Minutes*

*Serves: 4*

It's the perfect nibble when paired with fresh and luscious strawberries. These sugar-free, low-carb Keto chocolate-dipped strawberries are packed with the chocolate and berry sweetness you know and love.

**Nutrition**

Calories: 84 | Sugar: 1g | Fat: 4g | Fiber: 0g | Protein: 2g | Carbohydrates: 2g

## Ingredients

- 8 strawberries
- 1 teaspoon erythritol or stevia
- 2 oz 100% dark chocolate

## Instructions

1. Rinse and pat dry the strawberries.
2. In a double boiler, melt the chocolate and whisk in the sweetener.
3. Using a fork, dip each strawberry into the melted chocolate.
4. Place each chocolate-dipped strawberry on a dish lined with parchment paper. Refrigerate the chocolate until it has hardened.

# NO-BAKE KETO PEANUT BUTTER CHOCOLATE BARS

*Prep Time: 10 Minutes*

*Cook Time: 1 Minute*

*Chill Time: 60 Minutes*

*Serves: 8*

No-Bake Keto Peanut Butter Chocolate Bars will satisfy your sweet tooth while containing nearly no sugar. Peanut Butter Bars are a fantastic low-carb, low-sugar, high-fat keto dessert or fat bomb.

**Nutrition**

Calories: 246kcal | Carbohydrates: 7g | Sugar: 1g | Fiber: 3g | Protein: 7g | Fat: 23g

## Ingredients

### For the Bars

- ¼ cup Swerve, Icing sugar style
- ¾ cup Superfine Almond Flour
- ½ cup Creamy Peanut Butter
- 1 teaspoon Vanilla extract
- 2 oz Butter

### For the Topping

- ½ cup Sugar-Free Chocolate Chips

## Instructions

1. Combine all of the ingredients for the bars in a small 6-inch pan and spread evenly.
2. Microwave the chocolate chips for thirty seconds, stirring afterward.
3. If necessary, add another ten seconds to dissolve completely.
4. On top of the bars, spread the topping.
5. Refrigerate for an hour or two or until the bars have thickened. Keep in mind that these bars improve with age, so don't consume them right away.

# KETO BAGEL FAT BOMBS

*Prep Time: 10 Minutes*

*Cook Time: 0 Minutes*

*Chill Time: 30 Minutes*

*Serves: 18*

These Keto Bagel Fat Bombs are a tasty ball of bagel contents - cream cheese, smoked salmon, and chives - that you can eat in two bites! These savory snacks can also be served as a dessert

## Nutrition

Calories: 60kcal | Carbohydrates: 1g | Fat: 5g | Fiber: 0.2g | Sugar: 0.8g | Protein: 2g

Saturated Fat: 2g | Cholesterol: 15mg

## Ingredients

- ¼ teaspoon White Pepper ground
- 4 ounces Smoked Salmon chopped
- 8 ounces Cream Cheese softened
- 2 tablespoons Chives chopped
- ⅓ cup Everything Seasoning
- 1 teaspoon Dried Dill
- Salt to taste

## Instructions

1. In a mixing basin, beat the cream cheese with a hand mixer until smooth.
2. Combine the chives, dill, and pepper in a mixing bowl. On medium speed, beat for one-two minutes, or until smooth and fluffy.
3. Mix with the smoked salmon thoroughly.
4. Taste and season with salt if necessary.
5. Measure out bite-sized balls with a cookie scoop, set them on a prepared baking sheet, and refrigerate for thirty minutes.
6. On a plate, combine all of the seasonings.
7. Roll the fat bombs into a round shape one at a time, then roll them in the spice ingredients. To apply the seasoning to the balls, gently roll them in your hands.
8. Enjoy right away or keep refrigerated until required.

# BLACKBERRY COCONUT FAT BOMBS

*Prep Time: 5 Minutes*

*Cook Time: 5 Minutes*

*Chill Time: 60 Minutes*

*Serves: 16*

Low Carb and Paleo, these sugar-free blackberry coconut fat bombs are delicious. To stay in ketosis while losing weight on a ketogenic diet, eat them in between meals.

**Nutrition**

Calories: 170 | Fat: 18.7g | Carbohydrates: 3g | Fiber: 2.3g | Protein: 1.1g

## Ingredients

- 1 tablespoon lemon juice
- ½ cup fresh or frozen blackberries can use raspberries or strawberries if desired
- 1 cup coconut butter see note for how to make homemade
- ½ teaspoon Sweet Leaf stevia drops add a bit more for a sweeter taste
- ¼ teaspoon vanilla powder or ½ teaspoon vanilla extract
- 1 cup coconut oil

## Instructions

1. Heat the coconut butter, coconut oil, and frozen blackberries (if using) in a pot over medium heat until thoroughly mixed.
2. Mix the coconut oil mixture and the remaining ingredients in a food processor or small blender. Blend until completely smooth.
3. NOTE: If the coconut oil mixture is excessively heated, separation may occur. There's no need to boil the berries with coconut oil and butter if you're using fresh berries.
4. Refrigerate for at least one hour or until the mixture has firm.
5. Remove the squares from the container and cut them into squares.
6. Refrigerate until ready to use.

# KETO PINA COLADA FAT BOMBS

*Prep Time: 10 Minutes*

*Cook Time: 1 Minute*

*Chill Time: 60 Minutes*

*Serves: 16*

Our Low Carb Pina Colada Fat Bombs are a simple and delicious snack that tastes like classic. They'll transport you back to those delightful summer sensations. There's no need for sugar or alcohol.

**Nutrition**

Calories: 23kcal | Protein: 2g | Carbohydrates: 0.4g | Fat: 2g | Fiber: 0.1g | Sugar: 0.2g

Saturated Fat: 2g | Sodium: 5mg

## Ingredients

- 1/2 cup boiling water
- 1/2 cup Coconut Cream
- 3 teaspoons Erythritol
- 1 teaspoon rum extract
- 2 tablespoons gelatin
- 2 teaspoons pineapple essence
- 2 scoops MCT Powder Optional

## Instructions

1. In a heatproof container, dissolve the gelatin and erythritol in boiling water, then add the pineapple essence.
2. Allow five minutes for cooling.
3. Stir in the coconut cream and rum extract for another two minutes.
4. Pour into silicone molds and allow them to cure for at least one hour, depending on the size of the mold.
5. Remove the mold gently and serve. Keep refrigerated.
6. [Optional] If you want to amp. up the flavor of your fat bombs, consider adding a scoop or two of MCT Powder, but make sure to thoroughly mix it in hot water first, which may need the use of a stick blender.

# LOW-CARB CHOCOLATE MESS WITH BERRIES AND CREAM

*Prep Time: 15 Minutes*

*Cook Time: 20 Minutes*

*Serves: 16*

With whipped cream, almonds, and berries, it's a gourmet low-carb chocolate cake. On any celebratory occasion, a dessert like this is a surefire hit.

**Nutrition**

Calories: 357kcal | Protein: 5g | Fat: 33g | Carbohydrates: 9g

# Ingredients

## Dark chocolate cake

- 5 eggs
- 9 oz. dark chocolate with a minimum of 80% cocoa solids
- 5 oz. butter
- 1 teaspoon vanilla extract
- 1 pinch salt

## For Serving

- 6 tablespoons lime juice
- 4 oz. pecans, chopped
- 8 oz. fresh raspberries or fresh blueberries
- 2 cups heavy whipping cream or crème Fraiche
- 1 teaspoon vanilla extract
- 1½ oz. roasted unsweetened coconut chips

# Instructions

## Dark chocolate cake

1. Preheat the oven to 320 degrees Fahrenheit. Use a springform with a maximum diameter of 9 inches. Apply a thin layer of butter or coconut oil to the bottom of the mold and secure a piece of round parchment paper to the bottom.
2. Chocolate will be broken into bits, and butter must be diced. Melt the ingredients together in a double boiler or in the microwave. Chocolate can burn easily, so stir frequently. Allow it to cool once melted.
3. Separate the eggs into yolks and whites and place them in separate basins. Whisk the egg whites with the salt until firm peaks form. Set aside
4. Whisk the egg yolks with the vanilla extract until creamy.
5. Mix the melted chocolate and butter thoroughly into the egg yolks. In a separate bowl, whisk together the egg whites. Fold until no white streaks from the egg whites can be seen, but no more than that. Bake for fifteen-twenty minutes after pouring the batter into the mold. When it's done, test it with a knife to check whether it's ready. It shouldn't be runny, but it should be wet.

## For serving

1. In a small bowl, combine the berries, lime juice, and vanilla extract. Allow for a few minutes of rest.
2. In a large mixing bowl, beat the cream until soft peaks form.
3. With your fingers, divide the dark chocolate cake into bite-size pieces. Serve on individual serving plates.
4. Add the berries, then top with coconut flakes and nuts.
5. Serve with a dollop of whipped heavy cream or crème Fraiche on top right away.

# KETO BAKED GOAT CHEESE WITH BLACKBERRIES AND ROASTED PISTACHIOS

*Prep Time: 0 Minutes*

*Cook Time: 12 Minutes*

*Serves: 4*

This mouthwatering oven-baked goat cheese dish is equally great as an appetizer or dessert. But it's so delicious and healthy that you could have it for lunch with a good salad

**Nutrition**

Calories: 584 | Protein: 33g | Fat: 46g | Carbohydrates: 4g

**Ingredients**

- 1¼ lbs. goat cheese

Blackberry sauce

- 9 oz. fresh blackberries
- pinch ground cinnamon
- 1 tablespoon erythritol optional

Topping

- salt
- 1 oz. pistachio nuts
- fresh rosemary

**Instructions**

1. Preheat the oven to 350 degrees Fahrenheit
2. Combine the blackberries, cinnamon, and sweetener (if using) in a mixing bowl. Set aside.
3. Bake the goat cheese for ten to twelve minutes, or until it has developed some color. Remove from the oven and set aside for a few minutes.
4. Pistachios will be roughly chopped and roasted in a dry frying pan. Season with salt and pepper.
5. Blackberry, roasted pistachio and rosemary go well with goat cheese.

# KETO FRENCH PANCAKES

*Prep Time: 5 Minutes*

*Cook Time: 10 Minutes*

*Serves: 4*

These light-as-a-feather French pancakes, also known as crêpes, are ideal for breakfast, brunch, or dessert. For a satisfying keto dessert, the whole family will appreciate the top with berries and softly whipped cream.

**Nutrition**

Calories: 605kcal | Protein: 16g | Fat: 58g | Carbohydrates: 4g

**Ingredients**

- ½ cup water
- 8 large eggs
- 2 tablespoons ground psyllium husk powder
- 2 cups heavy whipping cream
- 1 oz. butter
- ¼ teaspoon salt

**Instructions**

1. Using a hand mixer, combine eggs, cream, water, and salt in a mixing dish.
2. While continuing to mix, gradually whisk in the psyllium husk until you have a smooth batter. Allow for at least ten minutes of resting time.
3. Pancakes will be fried with butter, just like conventional pancakes. 12 cup batter per pancake is a good estimate. Keep your frying pan on medium-high heat and make sure it's not too big or too hot.
4. Don't rush the process; wait until the top is nearly dry before flipping.

# LOW-CARB BAKED APPLES

*Prep Time: 5 Minutes*

*Cook Time: 15 Minutes*

*Serves: 4*

This quick and easy low-carb baked apple recipe comes together quickly. It smells like apple pie and tastes even better. Don't forget to top it off with a dab of whipped cream.

**Nutrition**

Calories: 341kcal | Protein: 3g | Fat: 33g | Carbohydrates: 7g

## Ingredients

- 4 tablespoon coconut flour
- 1 tart/sour apple
- ½ teaspoon ground cinnamon
- ¼ teaspoon vanilla extract
- 1 oz. pecans or walnuts
- 2 oz. butter, at room temperature

For serving

- ½ teaspoon vanilla extract
- ¾ cup heavy whipping cream

## Instructions

1. Preheat the oven to 350 degrees Fahrenheit. To make a crumbly dough, combine soft butter, chopped almonds, coconut flour, cinnamon, and vanilla.
2. Rinse the apple but leave the seeds and peel on. Both ends must be cut off, and the middle should be cut into four pieces.
3. Sprinkle dough crumbs on top of the slices in a greased baking dish. Bake for fifteen minutes or until golden brown crumbs is achieved.
4. In a medium-sized mixing bowl, whisk heavy whipping cream and vanilla extract until soft peaks form.
5. Allow the apples to cool for a few minutes before serving with whipped cream.

# OLD-FASHIONED KETO CAKE DONUTS

Prep Time: 10 Minutes

Cook Time: 20 Minutes

Serves: 8

In 30 minutes, you can make donuts that rival those from a professional baker! These old-fashioned keto cake donuts are topped with a lovely cream cheese icing and a smidgeon of chocolate drizzle. Try not to give in

**Nutrition**

Calories: 295kcal | Protein: 7g | Fat: 29g | Carbohydrates: 2g

## Ingredients

### Donuts

- 6 large eggs
- ½ cup butter or coconut oil
- ½ cup coconut flour
- ½ cup erythritol
- ¼ teaspoon baking soda
- ¼ teaspoon almond extract
- 1 teaspoon vanilla extract
- ¼ teaspoon sea salt

### Frosting

- ¼ cup cream cheese softened
- ¼ cup melted butter or coconut oil
- ¼ cup powdered erythritol
- 2 tablespoons powdered erythritol
- 1 tablespoon cocoa powder, unsweetened
- Chocolate drizzle
- ½ teaspoon vanilla extract
- 3 tablespoon melted butter

## Instructions

1. Preheat the oven to 350 degrees Fahrenheit
2. Combine the dry doughnut ingredients in a large bowl. Mix the wet and dry ingredients in a mixing bowl. Fill greased doughnut pan circles with batter until they are about 2/3 filled. Bake for twenty minutes, or until a toothpick inserted in the center comes out clean.
3. Meanwhile, make the frosting by mixing all of the ingredients together in a medium shallow bowl.
4. Chill cooled doughnuts by dipping them in frosting and placing them on parchment paper.
5. To prepare the chocolate drizzle, combine all of the ingredients in a small mixing dish and swirl well to blend. If desired, pour the chocolate drizzle over the doughnuts.

# SUGAR-FREE RASPBERRY CHOCOLATE SOUFFLÉ

*Prep Time: 10 Minutes*

*Cook Time: 10 Minutes*

*Serves: 4*

With pureed raspberries and a smidgeon of dark chocolate, this is a healthful treat. The raspberries add a lovely swirl of pink ribbons and a bit of sweetness. The chocolate in the middle is a delightful surprise.

**Nutrition**

Calories: 59kcal | Protein: 4g | Fat: 3g | Carbohydrates: 2g

**Ingredients**

- 4 large egg whites
- 1 2/3 tablespoon sugar-free baking chocolate chopped
- 2/3 cup fresh raspberries
- ¼ cup powdered erythritol
- 1 teaspoon unsalted butter

**Instructions**

1. Preheat the oven to 375 degrees Fahrenheit. Using butter, lightly grease one 3.5-inch ramekin for each serving. Set aside the ramekins on a baking sheet.
2. In a blender, puree the raspberries. You can strain the puree through a wire mesh or cheesecloth to remove the seeds if you desire, but it's not required.
3. Whip the egg whites in a separate bowl. Gradually add the sweetener when the whites begin to form soft peaks. Whip the cream until stiff, glossy peaks form.
4. Pour the raspberry puree around the egg whites on the bowl's sides. If you don't want the egg whites to deflate, don't pour directly on them. Gently fold the egg whites around the puree with a spatula, generating raspberry puree streaks in the egg whites.
5. Dollop the egg white mixture into each ramekin approximately halfway. The mixture must not be smoothed or pressed down. Fill each ramekin with the remaining egg white mixture after sprinkling 1/4 of the chocolate over each ramekin.
6. Bake on a lower oven rack for ten-twelve minutes, or until the soufflé has risen and is gently browned. Remove the dish from the oven and serve right away. As the soufflés cool, they will naturally deflate a little.

# LOW-CARB STRAWBERRY CREAM GUMMIES

*Prep Time: 30 Minutes*

*Cook Time: 30 Minutes*

*Chill Time: 60 Minutes*

*Serves: 4*

This no-bake Easter delicacy is simple to make and delicious! These pink delights will be the perfect dessert for your spring spread if you use any decorative silicone molds. This is a genuine gastronomic pleasure that you may enjoy.

**Nutrition**

Calories: 39kcal | Protein: 4g | Fat: 1g | Carbohydrates: 3g

## Ingredients

- ½ teaspoon liquid sweetener, stevia glycerite
- 2 tablespoon pastured unflavored powdered gelatin
- 7 oz. fresh strawberries
- ½ teaspoon vanilla extract
- ½ teaspoon lemons zest
- 1 pinch salt
- 1 cup unsweetened almond milk

## Instructions

1. In a blender, combine the berries and milk until smooth. To remove the seeds, strain the mixture through a fine-mesh screen.
2. In a saucepot over medium heat, warm the strawberry milk, then whisk in the stevia, vanilla, lemon zest, and salt. If desired, add more sugar to the milk.
3. Pour the milk back into the blender once it begins to steam. Blend on low for fifteen seconds after adding the gelatin. Pour the mixture into the silicone mold and chill for sixty minutes to solidify.
4. Remove the gummies from the fridge and unmold them once they have firmed up. Chill before serving.

# LOW-CARB GRANOLA BARS

*Prep Time: 10 Minutes*

*Cook Time: 20 Minutes*

*Serves: 20*

Nuts love seeds, seeds adore dark chocolate, and all of them adore coconut. When you mix all of those ingredients into healthy, low-carb granola bars, be prepared for a giant bear hug of flavor

## Nutrition

Calories: 190kcal | Protein: 5g | Fat: 17g | Carbohydrates: 3g

## Ingredients

- 2 large eggs
- 2/3 cup unsweetened finely shredded coconut
- 2 oz. dark chocolate with a minimum of 70% cocoa solids
- 3 oz. almonds
- 7 tablespoon pumpkin seeds
- 2 oz. sesame seeds
- 2 teaspoon ground cinnamon
- 1 teaspoon vanilla extract
- 4/5 cup walnuts
- 1 oz. flaxseed
- 6 tablespoon coconut oil
- 4 tablespoon tahini
- 1 pinch sea salt
- 3 oz. dark chocolate with a minimum of 70% cocoa solids for garnish (optional)

## Instructions

1. Preheat the oven to 350 degrees Fahrenheit (175 degrees Celsius).
2. In a blender or food processor, combine all of the ingredients until finely chopped.
3. Fill a 7 x 11" baking dish with the ingredients, preferably lined with parchment paper.
4. Bake for fifteen-twenty minutes, or until a golden-brown color has developed on the cake.
5. Allow it to cool slightly before removing it from the baking dish. Using a sharp knife, cut into 20 or 24 pieces.
6. Melt the chocolate in a double boiler over hot water or in the microwave.
7. Only around 0.5" or one side of each bar must be dipped in chocolate. Allow it to cool completely before serving.
8. Refrigerate or freeze the leftovers.

# SALTY CHOCOLATE TREAT

*Prep Time: 10 Minutes*

*Cook Time: 1 Minute*

*Chill Time: 70 Minutes*

*Serves: 10*

Chocolatey, coconut-tastic, and seed-a-rific. Yes, of course. We took this recipe with us. A low-carb snack made with dark chocolate and a plethora of nuts and seeds

**Nutrition**

Calories: 80kcal | Protein: 1g | Fat: 6g | Carbohydrates: 4g

## Ingredients

- 1 tablespoon pumpkin seeds
- 2 tablespoons roasted unsweetened coconut chips
- 10 hazelnuts or pecans or walnuts
- 3½ oz. dark chocolate with a minimum of 80% cocoa solids
- sea salt

## Instructions

1. Melt the chocolate in twenty-second intervals in a double boiler or in the microwave.
2. Bring out 10 mini cupcake liners with a diameter of no more than 2-inch
3. Fill the cupcake liners with chocolate.
4. Add nuts, coconut chips, seeds, and a few salt flakes at the end if you prefer a saltier flavor.
5. Allow it to cool before storing in the refrigerator.

# KETO BUÑUELOS

*Prep Time: 10 Minutes*

*Cook Time: 20 Minutes*

*Serves: 4*

For all intents and purposes, Buuelos is the Latin equivalent of a donut. The recipes differ widely from one location to the next! They are cooked with root vegetables in Cuba and with cheese in Colombia. We blended techniques and tastes to create a Buuelo that is both keto and delicious.

**Nutrition**

Calories: 479kcal | Protein: 17g | Fat: 42g | Carbohydrates: 5g

## Ingredients

- 2 large eggs
- 2 tablespoon ground psyllium husk powder
- 1 cup fine ground almond flour
- ¼ cup erythritol
- 7 oz. crumbled feta cheese
- 2 cups coconut oil
- ½ cup cream cheese
- 1 pinch ground nutmeg
- 1 pinch salt
- ½ teaspoon baking soda

## Instructions

1. In a 9-10-inch skillet, heat the oil over medium heat.
2. Whisk together the almond flour, psyllium husk, salt, nutmeg, baking soda, and erythritol in a large mixing dish.
3. Break up the feta with your hands and crumble it into the dry ingredients.
4. Fold in the cream cheese and eggs until they are completely mixed.
5. When a wooden spoon is inserted into the oil and sizzles, the oil is ready.
6. Form the mixture into 8 or more 2-inch balls. Drop each one into the hot oil one at a time. Because they expand when frying and you don't want to crowd the skillet, we cooked four-six at a time.
7. Cook for two-three minutes until browned, then flip with a slotted spoon and cook for another two minutes.
8. Remove the Buuelos from the oil and place them on a wire rack to cool while you continue to fry the remaining batter.
9. If desired, garnish with confectioner's erythritol. Take pleasure at the moment.

# LOW-CARB FROZEN YOGURT POPSICLES

*Prep Time: 10 Minutes*

*Chill Time: 120 Minutes*

*Serves: 12*

Joyful. Yes, of course. You'll be overjoyed with these low-carb popsicles! They're great for keeping cool in the summer and adding a splash of color in the winter. Plus, each popsicle has only 5g in total! Oh, sure.

**Nutrition**

Calories: 73kcal | Protein: 2g | Fat: 5g | Carbohydrates: 5g

## Ingredients

- 1 teaspoon vanilla extract
- 1 cup full-fat Greek yogurt
- ½ cup heavy whipping cream
- 8 oz. frozen mango, diced
- 8 oz. frozen strawberries

## Instructions

1. Allow ten-fifteen minutes for the mango and strawberries to defrost.
2. In a blender, combine all of the ingredients and blend until smooth.
3. Serve as soft-serve ice cream right away, or pour into popsicle molds and freeze for at least two hours. Of course, if you have an ice cream maker, you can use that.

# LOW-CARB CRANBERRY CREAM WITH PECANS

*Prep Time: 30 Minutes*

*Cook Time: 5 Minutes*

*Chill Time: 60 Minutes*

*Serves: 12*

While cranberries have a delightful traditional holiday flavor, many of us must be careful to restrict sugar, especially sugar found in fruit. This cranberry cream has a lot of healthy fat in it, so it has a great flavor and macros.

**Nutrition**

Calories: 189kcal | Protein: 2g | Fat: 17g | Carbohydrates: 5g

## Ingredients

1. 1 teaspoon unflavored powdered gelatin
2. 1 cup cream cheese, room temperature
3. ½ cup powdered erythritol
4. 2 oz. chopped pecans
5. 1 lb frozen cranberries
6. 1 teaspoon vanilla extract 1/3 cup water
7. 1 orange, the zest
8. ¼ cup mayonnaise
9. 1 cup sour cream

## Instructions

1. In a saucepan over low heat, combine the cranberries and water. Allow simmering until the cranberries have burst and are soft.
2. Remove the pan from the heat and add the gelatin, constantly stirring to avoid clumping.
3. Combine the sweetener, orange zest, and vanilla extract in a mixing bowl and stir until the sweetener is completely dissolved. Allow it to cool on the counter or in the refrigerator.
4. Whip the cream cheese with a hand mixer or a stand mixer. Mix in the sour cream and mayonnaise until completely combined and creamy.
5. Stir in the cooled cranberry sauce, orange zest, and chopped pecans with a rubber spatula. Fold until everything is well integrated.
6. Before serving, chill for at least an hour.

# LOW-CARB CHEESE PLATTER

*Prep Time: 15 Minutes*

*Cook Time: 0 Minutes*

*Serves: 10*

It's the season of giving. You enjoy having others around! But an hour before your visitors come, you're at a loss for what to feed them. Don't worry; we've got you covered. Watch those carolers drool after trying our wonderful low-carb cheese dish

**Nutrition**

Calories: 576kcal | Protein: 24g | Fat: 49g | Carbohydrates: 9g

## Ingredients

- 1¼ cups Edam cheese or other semi-hard cheese
- 5 oz. Gruyère cheese or comet cheese
- 5 oz. mozzarella, mini cheese balls
- 2/3 cup cream cheese
- 5 oz. parmesan cheese
- 5 oz. blue cheese
- 5 oz. Brie cheese

For serving

- 5 oz. pecans or other nuts of your liking
- 1½ cups celery stalks
- 2 pears
- 5 oz. butter
- 2 fresh figs

## Instructions

1. Pick your cheeses wisely, preferably organic and free of additives.
2. Choose from a variety of cheeses manufactured from different types of milk, such as cow, goat, or sheep's milk.
3. Choose different consistencies, ages, and sources for a variety plate.
4. When serving, make sure the cheese is at room temperature. So, for the best flavor, take the cheese out of the fridge a few hours ahead of time.
5. Add almonds, celery stalks, figs, pears, and any crunchy vegetables that you enjoy.

www.ingramcontent.com/pod-product-compliance
Lightning Source LLC
Chambersburg PA
CBHW081418080526
44589CB00016B/2582